PICTURE DICTIONARY

Tanvir Khan

V&S PUBLISHERS

MW00637538

Published by:

F-2/16, Ansari Road, Daryaganj, New Delhi-110002
☎ 011-23240026, 011-23240027 • *Fax:* 011-23240028
Email: info@vspublishers.com • *Website:* www.vspublishers.com

Branch : Hyderabad
5-1-707/1, Brij Bhawan (Beside Central Bank of India Lane)
Bank Street, Koti, Hyderabad - 500 095
☎ 040-24737290
E-mail: vspublishershyd@gmail.com

Follow us on:

For any assistance sms **VSPUB** to **56161**

All books available at **www.vspublishers.com**

© **Copyright:** *V&S* PUBLISHERS
ISBN 978-93-815881-9-2
Edition 2013

Printed at : Deep Colour Scan, Shahdara, Delhi-110095

Publisher's Note

The Picture Dictionary is an exciting interactive approach to vocabulary building for young learners. It offers everything needed to make learning a new language a delight.

Aim of the Picture Dictionary:

- To improve children's understanding of English
- To help children develop their dictionary skills
- To encourage children to enjoy learning English

Specifically designed to engage and motivate young learners and to make learing English a fun, the special features of the picture dictionary include: more than 500 words presented in alphabetical order; more than 500 coloured images; parts of speech; a sentence along with every word. In addition to these, 9 special sections on Animals, Birds, Electronics and Electrical Devices, Human Body, Flowers, Transport, Universe, Fruits, and Vegetables are also included. This picture dictionary introduces basic dictionary skills such as alphabetisation, spelling, pronunciation, and much more.

The A-Z pages allow children to learn about the alphabet and alphabetical order; find a word using the initial letter; check their own spelling; and learn how to use simple definitions of words. That will encourage the children to extend the vocabulary and to build up their knowledge of English words.

To Parents: Encourage children to look at the complete page and discuss with them what they can see. Encourage them to identify familiar and unfamiliar words.

We hope the dictionary will be acknowledged as a source to build word power and stimulate learning, especially among children.

Introduction

Unlike many other dictionaries, The Picture Dictionary not only contains words and its pictures, but also gives their meanings, parts of speech and uses of the words in simple sentences. This helps the reader relate to the words and also understand their usage.

Learning everything about words

What is Parts of Speech?

Every sentence has certain types of words in them. These words are divided into different kinds or classes according to their use, called "parts of speech". All these parts of speech serve a specific purpose in a sentence.

Every word in this dictionary has its part of speech written next to it. The parts of speech used in this dictionary are explained below:

Noun

Nouns are words that name a person, place, or thing.

Adjective

An adjective is a word that describes a noun.

Pronoun

A pronoun is a word that can be used in place of a noun to avoid repetition.

Verb

Verbs are also called "action words", as they describe what a person or thing is doing.

Adverb

An adverb is any word that gives us more information about a verb, another adverb, or an adjective. They tell us when, how, where, how much or how often.

Preposition

Words such as on, in, with and behind are prepositions. They show how one person or thing relates to the other.

Happy Learning...!! ☺

Aa

Apple
(noun)

a round-shaped, firm fruit

An **apple** a day keeps the doctor away.

Acrobat
(noun)

a person who entertains the crowd in a circus by doing difficult acts such as jumping, swinging and balancing in the air

The **acrobat** gave a beautiful performance.

Aeroplane (noun)

a vehicle that flies in the air, carrying people; has wings and one or more engines

The flight was delayed because of trouble with the **aeroplane**.

Airport
(noun)

a place where aeroplanes fly from and also land; also has facilities for the passengers of the aeroplanes

Juhu Aerodrome was India's first **airport**.

Alarm Clock (noun)

a table clock which rings at a set time to wake a person up

The loud sound of the **alarm clock** wakes up children for school.

Almond (noun)

an oval-shaped edible nut

Eating **almonds** everyday improves your memory.

Ambulance (noun)

a vehicle that carries people to and from hospital

After the accident, an **ambulance** carried the injured people to the hospital.

Aquarium (noun)

a glass box with water inside where fishes are kept

The Georgia aquarium in Atlanta, USA is the largest **aquarium** in the world.

Anchor (noun)

a device in the shape of a hook which is attached to a ship or a boat with a cable

An **anchor** is used to stop ships from moving.

Archer (noun)

a person who shoots arrows with a bow

Actor Geena Davis is a famous **archer**.

Ant (noun)

tiny crawling insects that live in large groups

Ants live in colonies.

Armchair (noun)

a big chair with support on both sides

Grandmother likes to sit on an **armchair**.

Apricot (noun)

a juicy fruit with a yellowish-orange skin

pricots are rich in Vitamin A.

A
B
C
D
E
F
G
H
I
J
K
L
M
N
O
P
Q
R
S
T
U
V
W
X
Y
Z

Armour (noun)

a hard metal covering used to protect soldiers and vehicles in a battle

A knight's **armour** is generally made of steel.

Audience (noun)

a group of people who come together to watch or listen to a scene, mostly a film or drama

The **audience** liked the clown's performance.

Army (noun)

a group of soldiers with weapons who are trained to fight a war and protect a country from enemies

The Indian **army** defeated the Pakistan **army** in Kargil war.

Award (noun)

a prize given to someone for doing good work

The soldier got an **award** for saving the children from drowning.

Astronaut (noun)

people who go to space

Neil Armstrong was the first **astronaut** to walk on the Moon.

Axe (noun)

a tool with a wooden handle and a metal blade

Woodcutters cut trees with an **axe**.

Athlete (noun)

a sportsperson who participates in track and field events

P.T. Usha was a great **athlete**.

Animals

Bear

Buffalo

Bison

Cow

Cat

Camel

Monkey

Fox

Deer

Dog

Jackal

Elephant

Giraffe

Lion

Horse

Mouse

Ox

Goat

Pig

Rhinoceros

Sheep

Hippopotamus

Rabbit

Stag

Lamb

Yak

Wolf

Zebra

a b c d e f g h i j k l m n o p q r s t u v w x y z

Bb

Ball (noun)

a round object used for playing; could be used in either football, cricket, tennis or any other sport

Sachin Tendulkar hits the **ball** so hard that it goes out of the field.

Baby (noun)

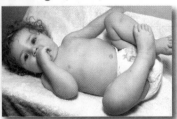

a newborn child who needs to be taken care of since he/she cannot do anything on his/her own

Sarah has given birth to a **baby** girl.

Banana (noun)

a yellow-coloured fruit which is eaten after taking the peel off

Eating **bananas** along with milk is very good for health.

Bangle (noun)

an ornament worn around the ankle or wrist by women

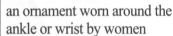

Bangles are usually made of glass or metal.

Bag (noun)

an object made of either plastic or leather or cloth or paper used to carry one's belongings

James carries a **bag** to school every day.

Basket (noun)

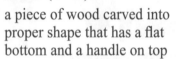

a container made of semi-hard material, used to carry objects

Mother took an empty **basket** to shop for fruits.

Balloon (noun)

an object that can be used for decoration or as toys for children; it is a small rubber tube that increases in size when air is blown into it

The house was decorated with **balloons** for Sam's birthday party.

Bat (noun)

a piece of wood carved into proper shape that has a flat bottom and a handle on top

Many sports such as cricket and baseball are played with a **bat**.

Bear (noun)

a wild animal found in a forest or a zoo

Bears have an excellent sense of smell.

Bulb (noun)

an electrical glass object which emits light when supplied with electricity

Thomas Edison invented **bulb**.

Bed (noun)

a furniture piece that is broad and has four legs; generally used for sleeping

Alan sleeps on his **bed** at night.

Burger (noun)

round but flat mass of meat or vegetables that is minced; generally fried and eaten in bread

Nancy treated all her friends to **burger** and chips on her birthday.

Bee (noun)

an insect which is popular for making honey; they are black and yellow in colour; they also make a buzzing sound while flying and their sting can be painful

Naughty Ray got stung by a **bee** when he threw a stone at the beehive.

Bus (noun)

a big vehicle used for carrying many passengers at one time

John, Nelly and Emma go to school by **bus**.

Bell (noun)

an electronic item that rings when a visitor presses a button outside the door of the house

On reaching Adam's house, Lisa rang the **bell**.

Butterfly (noun)

an insect that has a colourful body and wings

Butterflies fly in the day and suck nectar from flowers.

Bread (noun)

a common food item made of yeast, flour and water

Johnny enjoys eating **bread** with jam for breakfast.

Button (noun)

small objects sewn on clothing to hold them in place; it is stitched on shirts and trousers.

Polly's new dress has brass **buttons**.

Cc

Cat (noun)

an animal with fur; has a small tail and sharp claws

Rob's pet **cat** Furry is very naughty.

Cactus (noun)

a plant that has leaves; it has prickles all over and grows mostly in very hot places

Roots of the **cactus** plant are very close the surface so that they can absorb all the water from the rainfall.

Calculator (noun)

a small electronic device with a visual display and a keyboard to help you make mathematical calculations

The first electronic **calculator** was invented in the 1960s.

Camera (noun)

an object that uses a lens to capture photographs

Mark borrowed a **camera** from his friend to click photographs on his school trip.

Cage (noun)

a structure made of wires or bars to confine animals or birds in them

Animals in zoo are kept in large **cages**.

Candle (noun)

a block or cylider of wax, with wick it in the centre that is lit to produce light on burning

Mother lit a **candle** when there was an electricity cut.

Cake (noun)

a form of bread, sweet in taste which is generally cut to celebrate

Pat cut a chocolate-flavoured **cake** on his birthday.

Cap (noun)

a flat and soft hat that has a curved front end

Jamie is wearing a brown **cap**.

Car (noun)

a vehicle that runs on four tyres and can carry a small number of people from one place to another

The **car** is parked outside the house.

Coin (noun)

a metal chip, circular in shape, used as money to buy things

Jane loves to collect **coins** and has a huge **coin** collection.

Chair (noun)

a piece of furniture supported on four legs, used for sitting

Sammy got up from the **chair** and went towards the window.

Computer (noun)

an electronic device which takes in the user's instructions and stores and processes data, generally in binary form

Computers help in making our everyday lives easier.

Cheese (noun)

a solid milk product which is white or yellow in colour

Luke always tells mother to put extra **cheese** on his pizza.

Chocolate (noun)

a processed or raw food prepared mainly wih cacao seeds, which is either in the form of a solid block or a paste

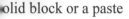

Father gave Anna a **chocolate** after she finished her homework.

Cottage (noun)

a small house where people live; usually in the countryside

Danny and his family spend their summer holidays in their **cottage** in the hills.

Coffee (noun)

a drink made by mixing milk and powdered coffee beans; can be hot or cold

Both father and mother have a cup of **coffee** in the morning.

Cup (noun)

an open top utensil which usually has handles; generally made of plastic or china

Mother serves tea to the guests in **cups** and saucers.

a b c d e f g h i j k l m n o p q r s t u v w x y z

Dd

Doll (noun)

a toy for children that resembles a small baby

Jane, Anna and Julie get together every day and play with their **dolls**.

Dance (noun)

a form of art wherein the body is moved in sync with the music

Alice's mother tells her the benefits of **dance**.

Dessert (noun)

a sweet dish that is eaten after a meal

Linda had a pastry for **dessert**.

Desert (noun)

an area of land, usually extremely hot that has none or very little rain, water, plants or trees

The Sahara Desert is one of the world's largest and hottest **deserts**.

Diamond (noun)

a precious stone that is bright, transparent and hard; used as a piece of jewellery

Father gave mother a **diamond** ring as a present.

Diary (noun)

a book that is used as planner; it has pages dedicated to everyday of the year separately

Glenda writes down all her class notes in her **diary**.

Desk (noun)

a piece of furniture that has drawers for keeping objects with a writing surface to read or write

Rob does his homework on the **desk**.

Dice (noun)

a cube with six sides on which numbers or dots from one to six are inked; generally used in board games

Amber rattled and threw the **dice** on the game board.

Dinner (noun)

the meal eaten in the evening

Robert had chicken and peas for **dinner**.

Drawer (noun)

a storage space in a desk or a table that can be locked

Ken opened Mary's **drawer** and took out a pen.

Doctor (noun)

a learned person who has knowledge about medicines and cures people who are ill

The **doctors** are looking at a patient's x-ray.

Dress (noun)

a single piece of clothing worn by girls that covers up till half the legs

The baby girl is wearing a pretty **dress**.

Dolphin (noun)

a friendly mammal that lives in the sea and looks like a very big fish; it has a pointed mouth

Dolphins are very intelligent and can learn tricks easily.

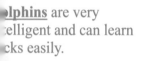

Drink (verb)

taking a liquid in the mouth and then swallowing it

Lisa **drinks** a glass of fresh juice in the morning.

Door (noun)

a huge glass, metal or wooden piece that is used as an entrance to a room or a building

The policemen broke the **door** of the robber's house.

Drum (noun)

a big musical instrument with two layers of skin attached to a round frame creating a hollow space in between.

Lee is learning how to play the **drums**.

Dragonfly (noun)

a brightly-coloured insect that is found near stagnant or slow flowing water

Dragonflies eat mosquitoes and other small insects.

Duck (noun)

a water bird that floats on water and has a big beak

Ducks eat a variety of things including fishes, grasses, insects, and even tiny worms.

Ee

Egg (noun)

a round or oval object which is laid by a female invertebrate, fish, reptile, or bird, that contains a developing new one

Mother gave me a boiled **egg** for breakfast.

Ear (noun)

body parts, one on each side of the head, used for listening

Danny whispered something in Lisa's **ear**.

Elbow (noun)

the joint between the upper arm and the forearm

Ben fell down and hurt his **elbow**.

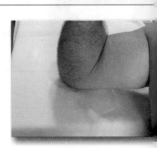

Earring (noun)

ornaments worn on the ears

Mother wore gold **earrings** to the party.

Elevator (noun)

a compartment or platform housed in a shaft to lower or raise people (or things) to different floors

Jane pushed the button for the fourth floor in the **elevator**.

Earth (noun)

the planet on which we live; the surface of the planet, distinct from the sea and sky

Earth is the only planet that has water.

Empty (adjective)

not occupied or filled; containing nothing

Judy drank all the milk and left the **empty** glass on the table.

Eat (verb)

the process of putting food in the mouth, chewing it and then swallowing it

Emma loves to **eat** a mango ice cream.

Engine (noun)

a part of any mechanical object that generates and provides power

[W]hen father turned the ignition on, the car's [en]gine roared to life.

Exercise (noun)

the movement of one body part or more with a purpose of getting healthy and fit

Mother tells me the importance of **exercise**.

[E]nvelope (noun)

[a] piece of flat paper, [wi]th a sealable [fla]p, folded in [a cer]tain way so that a [let]ter can be enclosed [wi]thin it

[An]dy sealed the letter [in] an **envelope** and posted in.

Eye (noun)

body parts located below the forehead which help us to see

On his birthday morning, Ray opened his **eyes** and saw that his room was full of gifts.

Eraser (noun)

a piece of rubber that is used to remove mistakes made while writing with a pen or a pencil

[Bo]b used an **eraser** to rub out his drawing.

Eyebrow (noun)

lines of hair that grow above each eye

Gordon showed Polly the scar above his right **eyebrow**.

[E]scalator [(n]oun)

[a] moving staircase [th]at is run by a motor [an]d has an endlessly [cir]culating belt of steps

[Gr]andmother took the [es]calator to the fifth floor [as] she could not climb the [sta]irs.

Eyelash (noun)

strands of hair that grow on the eyelids

Emily has very long **eyelashes**.

F f

Fish (noun)
an aquatic creature that has fins and a tail

Father caught several **fishes** from the pond.

Face (noun)
front side of the head where the nose, mouth and eyes are located; it begins at the forehead and ends at the chin

The baby has a nice and round **face**.

Feather (noun)
the covering on a bird's body; a lot of thin hair around a hard centre form a feather

A crow's **feather** is grey and black in colour.

Family (noun)

a group of people, usually parents and children, who are related to each other by blood

There are three people in Frank's **family**.

Foot (noun)
the body part located at the end of each leg which helps us to stand and walk

Jane injured her **foot** while dancing.

Fence (noun)
a boundary made from wood or wire to prevent unwanted people and animals from entering a particular space

Tom sat on the garden **fence** to enjoy the weather.

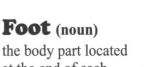

Fan (noun)
an electrical object that has a few blades which rotate to produce air in a room

Jen switched on the **fan** as soon as she entered home.

Finger (noun)
each of the four long thin parts the end of each hand

Mother wears rings on two of her **fingers**.

A B C D E F G H I J K L M N O P Q R S T U V W X Y Z

Fire (noun)

the bright, hot flames that are a result of something burning

A huge **fire** burnt the house down.

Forest (noun)

a huge land with dense trees

Many animals live in the **forest**.

Flower (noun)

plant's part that is usually colourful and as petals

he children gave ther beautiful **flowers** n his birthday.

Fork (noun)

an object used for eating food; generally has four metal pointers

Sam ate his dinner with a **fork** and knife.

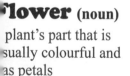

Flute (noun)

a thin wooden musical instrument used to produce tunes by blowing into the hole at one end

e plays the **flute** in the school band.

Friend (noun)

a person who is not connected by relations, but with whom one has a bond of mutual affection

Sally, Bella and Anna are best **friends**.

Fly (verb)

e controlled ovement of a rd or any other eature with ings through e air

rds **fly** up in the air.

Frying pan (noun)

a utensil with an open top that is used to cook food in oil

Mother prepared food in the **frying pan**.

Food (noun)

anything edible that is eaten to kill hunger

Mark enjoys eating Indian **food**.

Fur (noun)

the thick layer of hair on the bodies of animals

The dog has black and white **fur**.

a b c d e f g h i j k l m n o p q r s t u v w x y z

Gg

Gun (noun)
a type of weapon that is used to fire bullets

The robber showed a **gun** and entered the house.

Game (noun)
a sports activity in which you play against a team and try to win; it is a test of knowledge and skill

All the children were playing a **game** of hide-and-seek.

Girl (noun)
a female child

The **girl** is wearing a pretty pink dress.

Garden (noun)
a place in the compound of a house where flowers, vegetables and grass grows

Grandfather has a beautiful **garden** in his backyard.

Glass (noun)
a utensil made from transparen hard material and doesn't have a handle on the side

Ben raised the **glass** to his lips and had a sip of water from it.

Glasses (noun)
a pair of eyeglasses held together by a plastic or a thin metal frame

Both grandfather and grandmother wear **glasses**.

Gate (noun)
the main entrance to a house or a building

Bob opened the **gate** to the park and started walking inside.

Globe (noun)
the world is referred to as th globe

70% of the **globe's** surface i water.

Gloves (noun)

pieces of clothing that are worn over the hand till the wrist to protect the hand

Mary has a nice and warm pair of red **gloves**.

Golf (noun)

a sport where a sportsperson tries to hit the ball into holes in the ground using a stick

Tiger Woods is one of the best **golf** players in the world.

Grandparent (noun)

the parents of your parents

Steven spent his summer vacations with his **grandparents**.

Glue (noun)

thick sticky liquid stored in tube or bottle; it is used to tick two objects

evin stuck two pieces of aper with **glue**.

Grass (noun)

a commonly found plant with a lot of narrow green leaves; it is spread over a particular land

A football ground is covered with lush green **grass**.

Goggles (noun)

goggles are glasses that protect your eyes from water, wind, etc.

Jim wore his **goggles** in the swimming pool.

Grasshopper (noun)

a green-coloured insect with long and thin legs

Julie screamed when she suddenly saw a **grasshopper**.

Gold (noun)

precious metal ed for making naments and wellery

andmother has a lot of pretty **gold** jewellery.

Guitar (noun)

a musical instrument with strings which when moved, produce a tune

Ken is taking classes to learn to play the **guitar**.

Hh

House (noun)

a building where people live

Emma lives with her family in a beautiful red **house**.

Hair (noun)

strands that grow on the head

Karen a has very pretty golden **hair**.

Hang (verb)

suspend, or be suspended from above, with the lower part dangling loosely

Mother told Ben to **hang** the clothes on the rope to dry.

Hammer (noun)

a tool with heavy metal on one end and a handle at the other; used to push a nail into wall or wood

Father put a nail in the wall to hang a photograph with the help of a **hammer**.

Hanger (noun)

an object used for hanging clothes

Father always hangs his shirts on a **hanger**.

Hand (noun)

the end part of a person's arm beyond the wrist including the palm, fingers and thumb

Jude put his **hand** in his pocket and pulled out a handkerchief before sneezing.

Happy (adjective)

showing or feeling content and pleased

The baby is looking very **happy** to be with his mother.

Handle (noun)

a metal or wooden grip attached to a door and is used to open or close the door

The cupboard has a silver-coloured **handle**.

Hat (noun)

a shaped covering for the head which is usually worn either as part of a uniform, as a fashion item or to protect oneself from the weather

Peter wore a **hat** before going out in the sun.

Headphones (plural noun)

wires with padded earplugs used for listening to music or radio by wearing over the ears

David plugs in his **headphones** to the computer and listens to music all day.

Heavy (adjective)

a thing that has a lot of weight

The body builder is lifting very **heavy** weight.

Helicopter (noun)

a vehicle that can fly with a small number of passengers; it has blades on top that move very fast and help it fly

The **helicopter** is about to land.

Helmet (noun)

an object worn on the head to protect it from injury

Dave always wears a **helmet** while riding his motorcycle.

Hole (noun)

a hollow place in a surface or any other solid body

A huge stone fell from the lorry and made a **hole** in the road.

Horn (noun)

the hard and pointed things that grow on the head of an animal

The goat has very sharp **horns**.

Hot dog (noun)

a soft roll of bread with a hot sausage in between, topped with various condiments

Mother served the children **hot dogs** for lunch.

Housefly (noun)

a small insect with two tiny wings; generally found in the corners of a house that has sweets or dirt

Food should always be kept covered so that **houseflies** can't sit on it and contaminate it.

Hug (noun)

when a person puts his or her arms around the other person as a gesture of affection

Linda and Lisa are giving each other a **hug**.

a b c d e f g h i j k l m n o p q r s t u v w x y z

I i

Ice cream (noun)
a cold sweet edible item made by mixing crushed ice and frozen cream; it has different flavours too

Janet is eating a mix of both chocolate and vanilla <u>ice cream</u>.

Ice (noun)
a block of frozen water

Mother put a lot of crushed <u>ice</u> in the juice to make it cooler.

Instrument (noun)
a device or tool that is used to perform certain tasks

These <u>instruments</u> help doctors in curing a patient.

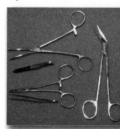

Iceberg (noun)
a huge ice mountain mostly found floating in the sea

A giant <u>iceberg</u> blocked the path of the ship.

Iguana (noun)
a reptile that looks like a huge lizard

The <u>iguana</u> is sitting on a log inside a glass cage.

Iron (noun)
an electrical device that has a flat base; is heated till the base becomes hot and then is rubbed over clothes to remove creases

Father <u>irons</u> his clothes every morning before getting ready for work.

Injection (noun)
a medical instrument with a needle at one end and a small tube at the other; used to inject medicine in one's body

Doctors gave the sick baby an <u>injection</u> to make him feel better.

Island (noun)
a land that is totally surrounded by water; piece of land in the middle of a water body

Hawaii is a chain of beautiful <u>islands</u>.

Birds

Cock

Cockatoos

Bulbul

Woodpecker

Crow

Crane

Cuckoo

Flamingo

Dove

Duck

Egret

Hummingbird

Hen

Hoopoe

Hornbill

Kiwi

Kingfisher

Koel

Mynah

Nightingale

Ostrich

Owl

Parrot

Sparrow

Skylark

Pigeon

Pelican

Vulture

Swan

Robin

Penguin

a b c d e f g h i j k l m n o p q r s t u v w x y z

Ji

Jam (noun)

a thick jelly-like food that is a sweet in taste; it is made by cooking fruit with a lot of sugar

Adam enjoys eating a butter and <u>jam</u> sandwich for breakfast.

Jacket (noun)

a piece of clothing worn over a shirt as a coat or to keep oneself warm

Emily wore a **jacket** before going out in the cold.

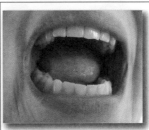

Jaw (noun)

the lowest part of the face

Ken fell down and broke his <u>jaw</u>.

Jaguar (noun)

a wild animal from the cat family; it has dark spots on its back

When not hunting, a <u>jaguar</u> sleeps.

Jeans (plural noun)

trousers made of denims

Vicky wears **jeans** and a t-shirt to office every day.

Jalapeno (noun)

an extremely hot green chilli pepper; generally used in Mexican cooking

Monica put a lot of **jalapenos** in her sandwich.

Jeep (noun)

a vehicle that has the capability to run on any kind of terrain

The family went in a **jeep** for a vacation in the mountains.

Jar (noun)

a container made of glass, which is used to store things

Mother kept all the chocolates in a <u>jar</u>.

Jelly (noun)

a transparent food to which artificial flavours are added

<u>Jelly</u> is generally eaten as a dessert.

Jellyfish (noun)

a type of fish that has clear body and has the ability to sting very badly

[W]hen naughty Ray put his hand in the [a]quarium, a **jellyfish** stung him.

[J]ewellery (noun)

[Or]naments worn by people [us]ually in the form of [br]acelets, necklaces and [ri]ngs

[Ju]lie bought a lot of gold [je]**wellery**.

Jigsaw (noun)

a picture puzzle; a picture is cut into various parts and placed [ra]ndomly which have to be arranged in the [co]rrect order

[K]im loves to arrange **jigsaw** puzzles to find out [w]hat the completed picture looks like.

[J]oy (noun)

[a] feeling [of] extreme [ha]ppiness or [pl]easure

[E]veryone can see [the] **joy** on the [ba]by's face while playing with balloons in the [ga]rden.

Joystick (noun)

a game controller with a lever that moves in all directions

Ben and Alice love to play video games with a **joystick**.

Jug (noun)

a utensil with an open top used to store and pour water

The **jug** is being filled with fresh orange juice.

Juggle (verb)

entertaining people by throwing things in the air, catching them and throwing them again, in such a way that there are many of them in the air at the same time

The jugglers are **juggling** bats.

Juice (noun)

the liquid derived from crushing fruits in a mixer

Lily is pouring orange **juice** in the glass.

Jump (verb)

Pushing yourself against the ground with the feet, and moving up towards the air

Bob is **jumping** in the garden.

K k

Ketchup (noun)

a spicy sauce made basically with tomatoes and vinega[r]

Sally ate her pizza with a lot of **ketchup**.

Karate (noun)

a fighting sport which is fought using legs, hands, elbow and feet

Dave and Mark are practicing **karate**.

Keyboard (noun)

an object used for typing and has all the alphabets and numbers, along with special characters

Father was typing on the **keyboard** when it suddenly stopped working.

Kennel (noun)

a small house made especially for a dog

The dog is sleeping in the **kennel**.

Keyhole (noun)

a hole in a lock where the ke[y] can be inserted

Dan peeped into David's house through the **keyhole**.

Kettle (noun)

a utensil that has spout and a handle and is used mostly for boiling water

Mother put the **kettle** on the stove to make some tea.

Kick (verb)

an action of hitting something or someone using feet

James **kicked** the ball.

Key (noun)

a metal piece with a specific shape used to open locks

Father keeps a spare **key** of the house in his drawer.

Kiss (verb)

touching someone with the li[ps] to show extreme affection

Sally gave her horse a loving **kiss**.

A B C D E F G H I J K L M N O P Q R S T U V W X Y Z

Kitchen (noun)

a room in the house that has arrangements for cooking

Father and mother cook food for the children in the **kitchen**.

Kite (noun)

a piece of paper tied with a thread and flown in the air with the support of the thread

The **kite** is flying high in the sky.

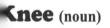

Kitten (noun)

a cat's baby or young one

The **kitten** is listening intently.

Knee (noun)

the part of body that joins the legs with the thighs

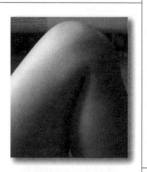

Alice fell down and bruised her **knee**.

Knife (noun)

a sharp metal object with a handle on one end, used for cutting objects

Mother uses a **knife** to chop vegetables.

Knight (noun)

a soldier who serves his king or queen in a battle

The brave **knight** saved the princess from a burning tower.

Knit (verb)

making a cloth using two sewing needles and thread or wool

Mother is **knitting** a pretty pink sweater for Julie.

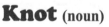

Knob (noun)

a round object attached to a door for opening and locking it

Naughty Ray pulled the **knob** so hard that it broke and fell off.

Knot (noun)

a fastening made by tying a piece of rope, cloth or any other similar material

The **knot** in Alex's lace couldn't be undone.

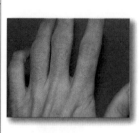

Knuckle (noun)

bones that protrude out when a finger or all fingers are bent

Mother couldn't take off her ring as her **knuckles** were swollen.

Ll

Ladder (noun)

iron or wooden stairs th can be taken anywhere

Jill climbed the **ladder** to reach the terrace.

Ladybird
(noun)

a small flying insect with a hard outer body; also has red and black spots on its back

Ron saw many **ladybirds** in his garden.

Laugh (verb)

expressing happiness or amusement by producing certain sounds

When Adam narrated a fun joke, Jane started to **laugh**.

Lamp (noun)

an object that emits light using electricity or by burning gas

The **lamp** lit up the huts at night.

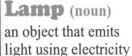

Leaf (noun)

the flat and thin parts of a plant or tree, which are generally green in colour

Lisa plucked a **leaf** from the branch of a tree.

Lantern (noun)

a metal lamp with glass sides and a handle on top

Mother hung a **lantern** outside the house at night.

Lemon (noun)

a small round yellow fru with flesh inside which when squeezed produce sour juice

Mother squeezed fresh **lemons** to make lemonade.

Laptop (noun)

a computer in the shape of a small briefcase; it is portable

Father gifted Nina a new **laptop** on her birthday.

Letter (noun)

a message written on a paper meant to be sent to someone far

Monica wrote a **letter** to her grandmother.

Lettuce (noun)

a green vegetable with big, layered leaves; generally eaten in salads

Mother puts a lot of lettuce and cucumber in her salad and sandwich.

Lipstick (noun)

a coloured substance in the shape of a stick used by women to apply colour to their lips

Mother applied a red **lipstick** to match the colour of her dress.

Lighter (noun)

a small plastic or metal object that has compressed fuel inside it, a knob on top helps it produce fire

Father lit the candles on Beth's birthday cake with a **lighter**.

Lock (noun)

an electronic or mechanical device that keeps a door, suitcase, etc., fastened

Mother always puts a **lock** on the door before leaving for work.

Lightning (noun)

a flash of natural light in the sky caused by the release of electricity

There was a lot of thunder and **lightning** yesterday night.

Log (noun)

a part of the tree's truck or any large branch that has fallen off the tree or has been cut off

Logs are used for construction work, as pulp for producing paper and as fuel.

Lip (noun)

the two outer edges of the mouth located below the nose

Ricky bit her **lip** while eating food.

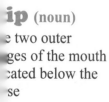

Luggage (noun)

trunks, suitcases and other bags in which personal belongings are packed while going for a tour

Father and mother had a lot of **luggage** on their way back from the vacation.

a b c d e f g h i j k l m n o p q r s t u v w x y z

Mm

Moon
(noun)

the round, white object that can be seen in the sky at night

There is no water on the **Moon**.

Machine
(noun)

an object that uses an engine or electricity to perform certain tasks that it is programmed to do

Joe sent an important document to his office using the fax **machine**.

Man (noun)

a grown-up male human being

The **man** is standing on the street.

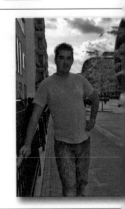

Magazine (noun)

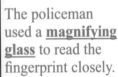

a booklet containing printed news, stories, advertisements, etc.

Kevin enjoys reading sports **magazines**.

Map (noun)

a map is the illustration of the globe on paper

Ted used a **map** to reach the museum.

Magnifying glass (noun)

a glass through which when an object is seen, it looks bigger than it actually is

The policeman used a **magnifying glass** to read the fingerprint closely.

Mask (noun)

an object worn over the face so that people cannot see who you are

Jen wore a scary **mask** to frighten her mother.

Matchstick

(noun)

the wooden portion of a match

Mother lit the stove with a **matchstick**.

Medal (noun)

a circular metal tied in a thread or ribbon given as an award for excellence in any field

The soldier won a **medal** for his bravery.

Melon

(noun)

a fruit that is round, has a thick yellowish skin and white flesh; also has seeds in the center

Melons grow in the summer.

Microscope

(noun)

an instrument used for making tiny objects look big, so that its details can be seen clearly

Scientists use **microscopes** to study various plants and animals.

Microwave oven (noun)

an oven that uses electromagnetic radiation for cooking food very quickly

Mother bought a new **microwave oven** from the market.

Milk (noun)

the white liquid that goats, cows and other animals produce; used by people as a drink and also for making cheese, butter and yogurt

Doctors recommend everyone to have two glasses of **milk** every day.

Mirror (noun)

a sheet of glass with a painted rear and is used to see one's own reflection

The cat gets confused whenever it sees its reflection in the **mirror**.

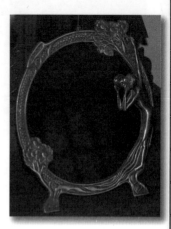

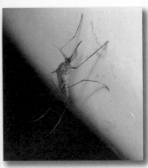

Mosquito (noun)

a flying insect that bites humans and animals to suck blood

Mosquito bites can cause various diseases.

Mountain (noun)

huge areas of rocky land and steep sides

Mount Everest is the highest **mountain** in the world.

Moth (noun)

an insect that looks like a butterfly but is less colourful

Moths are attracted to light.

Moustache (noun)

the bunch of hair that grows above the upper lip of males

Uncle Henry has a thick **moustache**.

Mouth (noun)

the part of body that has teeth, tongue and jaws

The dentist asked James to open his **mouth** wide.

Motorcycle (noun)

a vehicle with two wheels, an engine and seats for two persons

Ross wants to grow up and ride a **motorcycle**.

Mug (noun)

a utensil with an open top and a flat bottom; used to store and pour water

Jeff drinks a large **mug** of milk every morning.

Fruits

Almonds

Blueberries

Cantaloupes

Apple

Banana

Cashew nuts

Concord grapes

Graps

Chico fruit

Cherries

Coconut

Dates

Fig

Custard apple

Currants

Jackfruit

Jambu plam

Jujubes

Guava

Kiwi fruit

Litchi

Lemon

Grapefruit

Mango

Sweet lime

Muskmelon

Orange

Peach Pomegranate

Pineapple

Strawberry

N n

Nest (noun)

a place where birds live

A sparrow made its **nest** in a tree in Alice's garden.

Nail (noun)

a small metal object that is pointed on one end and flat on the other

Father drilled a **nail** in the wall to hang a painting.

Navy (noun)

the people of a country who fight at sea, using their ships.

Jamie's father is in the **navy**.

Nails (noun)

the hard and thin parts at the end of fingers of the hands and feet

Teacher told naughty Ray to cut his **nails** and keep them clean.

Neck (noun)

the body part that joins the rest of the body with the head

Giraffes have a very long **neck**.

Napkin (noun)

a small cloth or paper used for wiping hands or face

Ben put a **napkin** on his lap before eating dinner.

Necklace (noun)

a piece of jewellery worn around the neck

Rani wears a beautiful silver **necklace** to office.

Necktie (noun)

a narrow piece of cloth tied around the neck under the collar of a shirt

Father wears a **necktie** whenever he is going for a meeting.

Nib (noun)

pointed metal piece at the tip of certain pens which help in controlling the flow of ink

The pen has a golden-coloured **nib**.

Needle (noun)

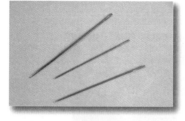

a very thin metal piece that has a small hole on one end through which a thread is put, used for sewing

Mother sew a button on Sara's dress with a **needle** and thread.

Night (noun)

the time when it is dark outside due to the setting of the sun; the time when people sleep

Owls stay awake during the **night** and sleep during the day.

Net (noun)

a piece of cloth sewn together by thick threads in a way that small hollow boxes are created

Mother puts a **net** around Beth's bed to protect her from mosquito bites.

Noise (noun)

any unwanted sound that is unpleasant

Rob was troubled by the **noise** in the market.

Noodles (noun)

curly, long yet thin strips of pasta; generally used in Chinese or Italian cooking

Steven had **noodles** and vegetables for dinner.

Newspaper (noun)

a bundle of papers with information and advertisements printed on it

Father reads the **newspaper** early in the morning.

Nose (noun)

the part of the body that helps us smell and breathe

Jack wiped his **nose** with a handkerchief.

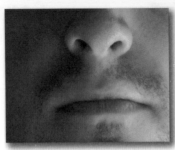

Number

(noun)

a value, which represents the quantity of a certain thing; also used for calculating, counting and to show the order in a series

The dice show the **numbers** 1 and 6.

Notebook

(noun)

a bundle of pages, pinned on one end; it is used for writing

Sam was ready with his **notebook** and pen before the teacher entered the class.

Nun (noun)

a female member of a religious community

Mother Teresa was a great **nun**.

Nursery

(noun)

a room in a house where the young child or children of the house play and sleep

Paul and his wife decorated the **nursery** even before their child was born.

Nozzle (noun)

a narrow piece that is fitted at the end of a pipe or a hose to control the flow of the liquid or gas

The **nozzle** is helping Mary control the flow of the water from the pipe.

Nut (noun)

fruit of some bushes or trees which is enclos in a hard shell

Nuts such as almonds, peanu and walnuts are good for health.

Vegetables

Fenugreek

Cucumber

Pumpkin

Radish

Corm

Potatoes

Sweet corn

Sweet potato

Ridge gourd

Spinach

Turnip

Tomato

Peas

Tinda

Yam

Arum

Bottle gourd

Beat root

Bitter gourd

Garlic

Coriander Leaves

Cabbage

Brinjal

Broccoli

Cluster beans

Chilies

Capsicum

Carrot

Cauliflower

a b c d e f g h i j k l m n o p q r s t u v w x y z

39

Oo

Owl (noun)

a bird that has a sharp yet small beak, a flat face and very big eyes

Owls stay awake during the night and hunt small animals for food

Oat (noun)

a cereal plant that is generally grown in cool climates and is consumed by both humans and animals

Eating **oats** for breakfast is considered very healthy.

Office (noun)

a room or a building where people go to work

Ned, Vicky and Henry are working in the **office**.

Ocean (noun)

a huge water body

The Pacific Ocean is the largest **ocean** in the world.

Oil (noun)

a thick yet smooth liquid that is made from plants and is used to cook food

Mother put some **oil** in the pan and fried some onions in it.

Odd (adjective)

a number which when divided by two leaves a remainder

9 is an **odd** number.

Olive (noun)

black or green in colour, bitter tasting fruits; generally used to make olive oil

Olives are generally used in Italian cooking.

Omelette
(noun)

a type of food item that is made by breaking eggs and cooking in a pan

Nick had a cheese **omelette** for breakfast.

On (preposition)

(in contact with, physically; supported by a surface)

Mother kept the vase **on** the table

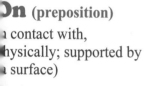

Open (adjective)

spread out; unfolded; something that is not closed and allows access

The book is lying **open** on the table.

Opposite
(adjective)

something that is on the other side

Both the players are standing on **opposite** sides.

Orchestra (noun)

a group of musicians who play various musical instruments together

The **orchestra** performed in front of a large crowd.

Origami (noun)

a craft in paper which is folded in a certain way to make different objects, people and animals, among other things

Nina learnt **origami** from her grandmother.

Ostrich (Noun)

an African bird that is very large in size but cannot fly

Ostrich is the largest living bird in the world and it also lays the largest eggs.

Overcoat (noun)

a warm, thick and long coat, usually worn during the winter months

The man is wearing a brown **overcoat**.

a b c d e f g h i j k l m n o p q r s t u v w x y z

P p

Pen (noun)

an object with ink inside it and is used to write

Jane wrote a beautiful poem with an ink **pen**

Paint (noun)

a coloured liquid that is applied on any surface for it to look good

The artist has mixed maroon and yellow **paint** together.

Parachute (noun)

an object that helps a person jump off an aircraft and land safely on the ground; it is a huge cloth with strings that are attached to the person's body

The man has a blue and white **parachute**.

Paintbrush (noun)

an object with a bunch of artificial hair on one end and a handle on the other and is used for painting

Paintbrushes come in various shapes and sizes.

Pastry (noun)

a sweet food made from bread and cream

Ken enjoys eating chocolate **pastries** with ice cream.

Palace (noun)

a huge house built in a large space; it was mainly referred to the houses of kings

The Queen of England lives in Buckingham **Palace**.

Peacock (noun)

a large beautiful bird that has a huge colourful tail that it spreads out as a fan

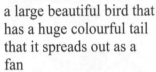

Peacock is India's national bird.

Pearl (noun)

a hard round object, usually creamy white in colour

Jason bought a beautiful **pearl** necklace for his mother.

Perfume (noun)

a liquid stored inside a bottle and is sprayed on one's clothes and body for fragrance

Mary applies **perfume** before leaving the house.

Pet (noun)

an animal kept in house for pleasure or company

Maggie's **pet** dog is called Oscar.

Piano (noun)

a musical instrument with white and black keys which when pressed in a particular sequence produces tunes

Colin plays the **piano** very well.

Pistachio (noun)

an edible green, small nut

Pistachio is basically a desert plant.

Play (verb)

spending time with someone while doing enjoyable activities

Alice and Julie are **playing** on the beach.

Pot (noun)

a utensil used for cooking food

Mother is making vegetable soup in a **pot**.

Qq

Question mark (noun)

a punctuation mark that represents a question

What is your name?

Quarry (noun)

a large place or a deep pit from where materials such as stones are taken out

Mark works in a limestone **quarry**.

Quilt (noun)

a warm bed covering made of padding enclosed between layers of fabric and kept in place by lines of stitching, typically applied in a decorative design

Father bought a beautiful blue **quilt** for Kevin.

Quiz (noun)

a knowledge-based test, generally given to students

All the students participated in the **quiz** competition.

Quick (adjective)

doing something in a very short time or moving very fast

Bob is **quick** to make friends.

Human Body

A B C D E F G H I J K L M N O P Q R S T U V W X Y Z

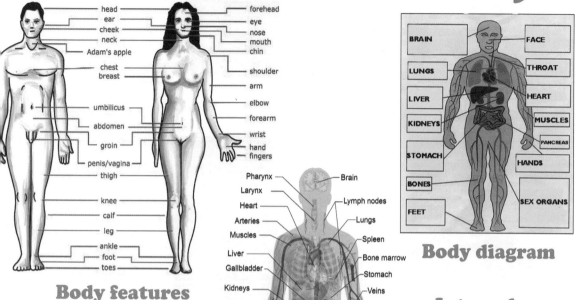

Body features

Body diagram

Internal organs

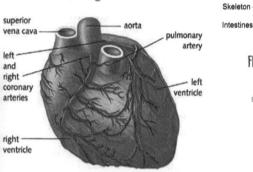

Coronary blood vessels

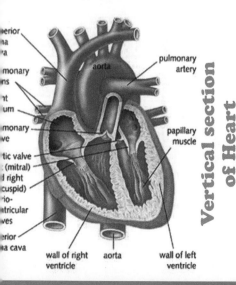

Vertical section of Heart

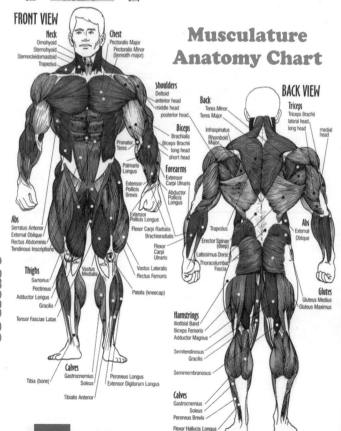

Musculature Anatomy Chart

A B C D E F G H I J K L M N O P Q R S T U V W X Y Z

Rr

Radio (noun)

a device that broadca[sts]
programmes

The news is broadcas[t]
on the **radio** every
hour.

Raft (noun)

a small boat made
of logs or other
materials for
floating on water

Due to the strong
current, the **raft**
turned over.

Racket (noun)

a bat that is oval in shape
and has strings across it

Rackets are used in variou[s]
sports such as badminton,
squash and tennis.

Rain (noun)

the small
drops of
water that
fall from
the sky

The car got
stuck in
heavy **rains**.

Read (verb)

looking at
something that
is written and
understanding it

Robbie **reads** the
newspaper every day.

Rainbow

(noun)
the multi-coloured
arch in the sky
spotted when it
rains

After the heavy rain, the sun came out and a
beautiful **rainbow** appeared in the sky.

Refrigerator

(noun)

a cupboard-shaped
electrical appliance that
keeps food and drinks co[ld]
and fresh

Refrigerators are usuall[y]
kept close to the kitchen

Remote control (noun)

a small rectangular-shaped object that controls electrical appliances from a distance

Vicky pressed the button on the **remote control** and changed the TV channel.

Ribbon (noun)

narrow iece of loth, usually oloured, that used for ecoration

ate tied her air with a retty red ibbon.

ice (noun)

e white or brown grains found in cereal plants

nny had **rice** and vegetables for dinner.

Ring (noun)

an ornament made of a precious metal and is worn around a finger

Mother wears a beautiful diamond **ring**.

Road (noun)

a strip of surface laid down for people to drive from one place to another

The policeman scolded naughty Ray for running on the **road**.

Robot (noun)

a machine that resembles a human being; it is a programmed machine and does things automatically

Robots are sent to space to help us learn more about it.

Rock (noun)

the hard substance of which the earth is made of

Justin tripped on a **rock** and fell down.

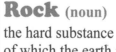

Rocket (noun)

a tube-shaped vehicle with a conical nose that is meant to travel into space

Rockets are launched into space to learn more about the world around us.

Rubber band (noun)

a thin elastic rubber, used to keep objects together

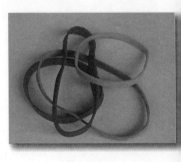

All the papers were tied with a **rubber band** so that they don't get lost.

Roof (noun)

the top part of a building

Mary's house has a red-coloured **roof**.

Ruler (noun)

an object that is used to measure the length, width and breadth of any object

Rulers are also used to draw straight lines.

Room (noun)

a space covered by walls on all sides and a ceiling

Jack put all his toys in the play **room**.

Rope (noun)

a very thick thread or wire that is made by twisting numerous thin threads or wires

The police tied the robber's hands with a thick **rope**.

Run (verb)

moving quickly, faster than walkin

The athlete is **running** in the field.

Universe

Earth

Sun

Moon

Comet

Asteroid

Milky way galaxy

Satellite

Rocket

Solar-system

Spacecraft

Ss

Spoon (noun)

a metal object with a straight handle on one end and a shallow curve at the other; used for eating food

Rob ate all the vegetables in the plate with a **spoon**.

Sad (adjective)

a state of mind when a person is unhappy

The baby is very **sad**.

Salt (noun)

a tiny crystal-like substance used to add taste to food

Grandfather puts a lot of **salt** in his food.

Seat belt (noun)

a type of belt attached to a seat in an aircraft or a car which is fastened across your body to make sure that  you are not thrown out of your seat in case of an accident or any sudden movement

Jerry met with a car accident, but was not hurt only because he was wearing a **seat belt**.

Sand (noun)

extremely small pieces of stones, mostly in a state of powder

Sand forms deserts and beaches.

Salad (noun)

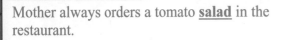

a mixture of some vegetables like cucumber, tomato, radish, lettuce, carrot, etc.

Mother always orders a tomato **salad** in the restaurant.

Sandwich (noun)

a food item that has meat, vegetables or cheese between two bread slices

Jim made himself a cheese **sandwich**.

Scarf (noun)

a small cloth worn over the head or around the neck

The lady is wearing a beautiful pink **scarf** around her neck.

Shark (noun)

an extremely large fish with very sharp teeth;

Sharks have many sets of replaceable teeth.

School (noun)

place where children go to study

The children go to **school** from Monday to Saturday.

Shoe (noun)

objects worn on the feet; they usually cover a major portion of your foot and are generally worn over stockings or socks

Father bought a nice pair of leather **shoes** for himself.

Scissors (plural noun)

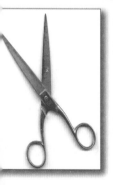

a tool with two blades screwed together; used for cutting things like cloth or paper

Jenny took out a pair of **scissors** from the drawer.

Seed (noun)

plant's small and hard part from which new plant grows

Alice planted some **seeds** in the soil.

Ski (noun)

narrow, flat and long pieces of plastic, metal or wood that are fastened to boots to help one move on water or snow

Uncle Jay is wearing a pair of wooden **skis**.

Sleep (noun)

natural state in which the mind does not have any thoughts, the body does no work or have much movement and the eyes are shut

The mother put the baby to **sleep**.

Slice (noun)

a piece of something that has been cut from the whole or a larger piece

Father'cut himself a **slice** of bread.

Smile (verb)

an expression a person gives when he or she is happy

When baby Ben saw the camera, he started to **smile**.

Snow (noun)

snow is formed by lot of soft, tiny frozen water drops

The **snow** covered all th trees in the park.

Soap (noun)

an object used for cleaning oneself while bathing; also used for washing clothes

Samantha uses a bar of rose **soap** to take a bath every morning.

Stethoscope (noun)

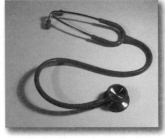

a tool used by doctors to count the pulse rate and breathing of a person

When Don fell ill, the doctor put a **stethoscope** to his chest to listen to his heartbeat.

Suitcase (noun)

a portable box with a hard outer covering and a handle in which clothes and other necessary items are kept, mostly during travelling

Father packed his **suitcase** the day before he had to leave for a trip.

A B C D E F G H I J K L M N O P Q R S T U V W X Y Z

Transport

Aeroplane

Bus

Bullet Train

Car

Hero Honda Scooty

Hero-Jet-cycle

Metro train

Indian train

F1 - Car

Rickshaw

Yamaha Bike

Jeep

a b c d e f g h i j k l m n o p q r s t u v w x y z

T t

Tea (noun)

a hot beverage made adding hot water to te leaves

Both mother and fath have a cup of **tea** wit their breakfast.

Table (noun)

a piece of furniture made of wood, used for reading and writing

Bob has a beautiful **table** in his room.

Taxi (noun)

a car that can be used by the public in exchange for money

Father called a **taxi** for a ride to the airport.

Tail (noun)

the extended part beyond the body of a fish, bird or animal

The horse's **tail** is has golden hair.

Teacher (noun)

a person who teaches at a school or colleg

The **teacher** taught the children how to paint.

Tap (noun)

an object through which water flows; it also has a knob through which the flow of water can be controlled

Beth turned on the **tap** to wash her hands.

Telephone (noun)

a device which helps you contact people in any corner of the world

Alice and Mary talk for hours over the **telephone**.

Television (noun)

an electrical appliance with a glass screen on which people see programmes or films with sound and picture

Grandfather enjoys watching the evening news on the **television**.

Tent (noun)

a leather or plastic material that is hung on various bamboos to form a temporary house

The family stayed in a **tent** when they went on a picnic to the hills.

Thermometer (noun)

a device used to measure the body temperature

The doctor used a **thermometer** to check if Sam had fever.

Thread (noun)

a thin piece of any material such as silk, cotton or nylon that is used to sew

Julie's dress was embroidered with beautiful golden **threads**.

Thumb (noun)

the thick and short extension on the side of the hand, next to the fingers

Jack fell from his bicycle and injured his **thumb**.

Tie (verb)

to fasten or bind together with a knot

The policemen **tied** the robber's hands.

Toast (noun)

a slice of bread that has been cooked at a high temperature due to which it becomes crisp and brown

Benny eats a **toast** with honey before going to school.

Tongue (noun)

the soft part of body present inside the mouth, which helps you speak, eat and taste

Kevin licked the ice cream with his **tongue**.

Train (noun)

a mode of public transport with bogies in which people travel; it runs on rails

Kelly and Ken travelled to their grandparent's house by **train**.

a b c d e f g h i j k l m n o p q r s t u v w x y z

Uu

Umbrella (noun)

an object used for protection from rain

Mother told Beth to carry an **umbrella** to school as it was raining.

Unicycle (noun)

a cycle with only one tyre and no handle

The clown was riding a **unicycle** in the circus.

Uniform (noun)

a set of special clothes worn by all the people of an organization, etc.

The children wear a grey and white **uniform** to school.

Up (adverb)

moving away from the ground, or moving towards the sky

Hot air balloon go high **up** in the air.

Use (verb)

to do something with a machine, an object, a method, etc., for a particular purpose.

The child is trying to **use** the mobile phone.

Utensil (noun)

objects that help to cook

Mother went to the market to buy new **utensils**.

Electronics & Electrical devices

Air Conditioner

Aquaguard

Black ipod

Ceiling fan

Cooking Range

Hair Dryer

Tube light

Juicer and mixer

Lamp

Microwave

Radio

Music system

Calculator

Mobile phone

ir Cooler

Vacuum cleaner

Television

Table Fan

Rafrigerator

Telephone

a b c d e f g h i j k l m n o p q r s t u v w x y z

V v

Violin (noun)

a musical instrument wit strings against which a bow is moved to produc a melodious sound

Dan has joined violin classes.

Van (noun)

a vehicle that has front seats and empty space behind to carry goods

The new television set that Father ordered was delivered in a **van**.

Vase (noun)

a vase is a flower holder usually made of glass

Uncle Sam bought a beautiful **vase** from England.

Vehicle (noun)

a machine that has an engine and space for passengers, in which people travel

A lot of **vehicles** on the road cause traffic jams.

Vegetable (noun)

a plant or its part that is eaten as food

Eating green **vegetables** is good for health.

Volcano (noun)

a mountain from which molten rocks and lava from inside the earth erupt.

The islands of Hawaii are a cha of **volcanoes**.

Volleyball (noun)

volleyball is a game played by two teams across a net in which a large ball is hit by hands. The two teams try and score points by making the opposite team mis-hit or not hit the ball.

The man is playing **volleyball** on the beach.

Flowers

Pink rose

Christmas cactus

Fritillaria Meleagris

Blue Flowers

Acacia

Holiday cactus

Paint Brush Flower

Cymbidium

Gaillardia pulchella

Lotus

Lantana Pink Caprice Microwave

Narcissus

Marigold

Red-camellia

Shamrock

Red Rose

Onastclose flower

Tulip

Redbud

Sun Flower

Orange flower

Peony

Orchid

a b c d e f g h i j k l m n o p q r s t u v w x y z

Ww

Watch (noun)

a small clock which has leather or chain strap and is worn on the wrist

Father bought Nate a **watch** for his birthday.

Wall (noun)

the vertical concrete side of any room or building

Father painted the **walls** of the room orange.

Water (noun)

a liquid used for drinking, cleaning and washing; it has no colour or taste

Jen was so thirsty that she drank four glasses of **water**.

Wallet (noun)

an object made of plastic or leather which is used to keep bank cards and notes

Father keeps a lot of money in his **wallet**.

Waterfall (noun)

a place in the mountains or hills from where water flows down into a pool

The Angel Falls is the world's highest **waterfall**.

Washing machine (noun)

a machine that uses electricity to wash clothes automatically

Father and mother wash all the clothes in the **washing machine**.

Wave (noun)

a large mass of water, which has been raised on the surface of the water; caused by either the tides or by winds that result in the rising and falling of a water body, usually in sea

A huge **wave** hit the shore.

Web (noun)

a net made by a spider using a sticky substance that it produces

The spider made a huge **web** in the orner of the window.

Wheel (noun)

round object that otates on an axle; t can have rubber trips around it nd fixed below a ehicles to help in ove to and fro

bicycle has two **wheels**, while a car has four.

Whistle

(noun)

an object that produces a loud and sharp sound when air is blown into it

he dog came running when his master blew e **whistle**.

Windmill (noun)

tower with ooden blades at rotate ith the wind d convert power into ectricity

he main purpose behind developing **windmills** as to mill grains.

Window (noun)

an opening in a room through which light and fresh air comes in

Mother opened the **window** to let some fresh air in.

Wing (noun)

the two parts of an insect's or a bird's body that help it fly

The bird spread out its beautiful **wings** and flew away.

Wire (noun)

a strong wire made of metal that has points sticking out of it; used to make fences

The prison was surrounded by **wires**.

Woman (noun)

a grown-up female human being

The **woman** in the picture is 31-years-old.

Wool (noun)

a thread made from the fur of sheep; used to make warm clothes and blankets

Grandmother knit a sweater for Kevin with **wool**.

a b c d e f g h i j k l m n o p q r s t u v w x y z

ABCDEFGHIJKLMNOPQRSTUVWXYZ

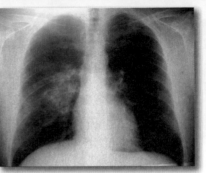

X-ray (noun)

a special photograph of inside the body

X-rays are used by doctors to check for injuries and sickness.

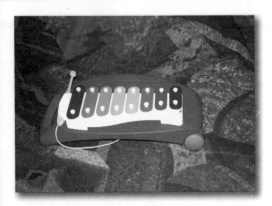

Xylophone (noun)

a musical instrument made of wooden or metal bars; these bars are hit with beaters to produce sounds

Lee is learning how to play the **xylophone**.

X-Mass Tree (noun)

a decorated evergreen tree related to the celebration of Christmas

Mother decorates a **x-mass tree** to celebrate Christmas.

Xerox (noun)

a machine that produces copies of letters, documents, etc.

Bob is trying to use the **xerox** machine.

Yy

Yak (noun)

a huge wild ox that is domesticated, with humped shoulders, big horns and shaggy hair

The **yak** is eating grass.

Yacht (noun)

a medium-sized boat with a cabin

Father bought a new **yacht** so that he could take Ben fishing.

Yawn (noun)

an involuntary action in which one opens his mouth and takes a deep breath

The dog began to **yawn** as soon as he sat down in the garden.

Yard (noun)

piece of nd next to house or a uilding

he house as a small ut beautiful ard.

Yogurt (noun)

creamy and thick food made from milk

Various fruits are added to **yogurt** to make it taste better.

Yarn (noun)

spun thread which is used for sewing, weaving and knitting

Grandmother spins the **yarn** d knits sweaters for her family for the winters.

Yolk (noun)

the yellow portion of an egg, which is rich in fats and proteins

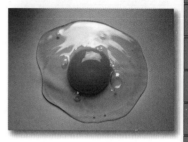

Mary enjoys eating the **yolk** of an egg.

Zz

Zebra (noun)

an animal that looks like a horse and has white and black stripes on its body

<u>Zebras</u> are generally found in Africa.

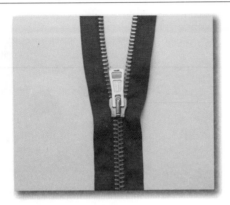

Zipper (noun)

a device consisting of two flexible strips of metal or plastic with interlocking projections closed or opened by pulling a slide along them, used to fasten garments, bags, and other items

Dave broke his jacket's <u>zipper</u> by mistake.

Zoo (noun)

an establishment that has a collection of wild animals for either conservation or display to the public

Father took the children to the <u>zoo</u>.

Zoology

(noun)

the scientific study of animals

Rob wants to study <u>Zoology</u> in future.

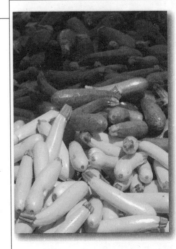

Zucchini

(noun)

a summer squash with a smooth skin

<u>Zucchini</u> cannot be eaten raw and should be cooked properly before eating.